Hospitality & Recreation

Careers for Today
Hospitality & Recreation

Marjorie Rittenberg Schulz

Franklin Watts

New York • London • Toronto • Sydney

Developed by: 𝛀 Visual Education Corporation
Princeton, NJ

Cover Photography: Marty Reichenthal/The Stock Market

Photo Credits: p. 3 Marty Reichenthal/The Stock Market; p. 6 Marriot
Corporation; p. 14 J.A.P./Bavaria/H. Armstrong Roberts; p. 18 Marriot
Corporation; p. 20 Texas Highway Magazine; p. 23 Michal Heron/Woodfin
Camp & Associates, Inc.; p. 26 Bob Hahn/Taurus Photos; p. 30 Lester Sloan/
Woodfin Camp & Associates, Inc.; p. 32 Marriot Corporation; p. 36 Robert
Bruschini/Hyatt Regency, Princeton; p. 38 Jonathan E. Pite/International
Stock Photo; p. 42 Robert Bruschini/Hyatt Regency, Princeton; p. 44 Robert
Bruschini/Hyatt Regency, Princeton; p. 47 Earl Dotter; p. 50 Robert
Bruschini; p. 53 Tami Campanella/The Club at Woodbridge; p. 56 Earl
Dotter; p. 59 Gerd Ludwig/Woodfin Camp & Associates, Inc.; p. 62 National
Restaurant Association; p. 65 Robert Bruschini; p. 68 Robert Bruschini/
Hamilton High School East; p. 72 Robert Bruschini/Lower Bucks Family
YMCA; p. 74 Robert Bruschini/Hyatt Regency, Princeton; p. 78 National
Association; p. 80 Robert Bruschini/Hyatt Regency, Princeton

Library of Congress Cataloging-in-Publication Data

Schulz, Marjorie Rittenberg.
Hospitality and recreation/Marjorie Rittenberg Schulz.
p.   cm. — (Careers for today)
Includes bibliographical references (p.   ).
Summary: Describes various careers available in recreation and hotel services
and provides suggestions for students interested in obtaining such work.
ISBN 0-531-10973-9
1. Hospitality industry — Vocational guidance — Juvenile literature.
2. Recreation leadership — Vocational guidance — Juvenile literature.
[1. Hospitality industry — Vocational guidance. 2. Recreation leadership —
Vocational guidance. 3. Vocational guidance.] I. Title. II. Series: Schulz,
Marjorie Rittenberg. Careers for today.
TX911.3.V62S38   1990
647.94′023 — dc20   90-12240 CIP AC

Contents

Introduction

Joey Barrici is four years old and afraid of the water. His father wants him to learn to swim. Whom does he call?

It's Thursday. The manager of the Rolling Hills Resort hotel has a flooded golf course. She has 200 people arriving on Sunday for a convention. Whom does she call?

Both of these people will look to workers from the hospitality and recreation field to help them. Mr. Barrici will call a swimming instructor at the local community pool. The resort owner will call her landscaping service to send a team of groundskeepers out as soon as possible.

Workers in hospitality and recreation have one main job: to help people relax and enjoy themselves. The field is divided into three main industries:

- Hotels and motels
- Food service
- Fitness and recreation

But these three industries are related to each other. A vacationer may travel to a ski resort (the fitness and recreation industry). While there, the skier will stay at a hotel and eat at the area's restaurants.

Hospitality and recreation is a growing field. As Americans enjoy more and more leisure time, they spend more and more money on the services of workers in these three industries.

Hospitality and Recreation Today

Currently, the field of hospitality and recreation is a large one. Hotels employ about 1.7 million workers. Another 7 million work in food service. And 1 million or so work in fitness and recreation. Put them all together, and you have almost 10 million workers—about the population of Florida.

The industry is important in another way, too. Many workers—whatever their later careers—begin their working lives in these industries. Waiting on tables, busing tables, or washing dishes are common part-time or summer jobs. Through this work, people learn basic job skills.

Workers in these fields, even part-timers, learn a valuable skill—how to treat customers. The U. S. economy is changing to focus more and more on service jobs. These are jobs in which workers do things for customers, rather than jobs in which they make goods. The way to have a happy customer is to provide good service. Hotel, food service, or fitness workers often deal directly with customers. This gives them the chance to see how their actions affect the customer.

They can learn this in another way, too. Workers in these jobs can supplement their income by earning tips. The better the service, the larger the tip a customer pays.

Trends in Hospitality and Recreation

Experts try to predict future trends or patterns for industries. Some important trends are expected in hospitality and recreation:

8

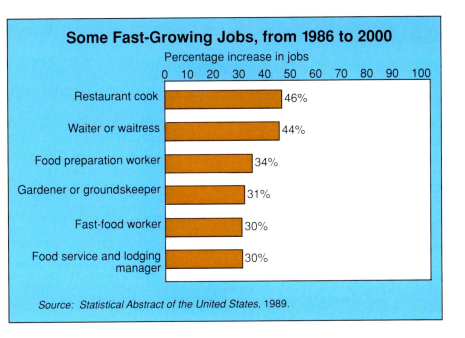

Some Fast-Growing Jobs, from 1986 to 2000

Percentage increase in jobs

Job	Percentage
Restaurant cook	46%
Waiter or waitress	44%
Food preparation worker	34%
Gardener or groundskeeper	31%
Fast-food worker	30%
Food service and lodging manager	30%

Source: Statistical Abstract of the United States, 1989.

- People will earn more and thus spend more on recreation.
- People will eat out more often.
- Convenient, affordable travel will help boost the hotel, motel, and restaurant business.
- The emphasis on health and fitness will continue, calling for more jobs.
- Businesses will add training programs in customer service and communications.

As a result of these trends, the outlook for jobs in hospitality and recreation is very good as we near the year 2000. The number of jobs is expected to grow to about 11.5 million

As the bar graph shows, the fastest-growing jobs in the future will be for restaurant cooks and

9

waiters and waitresses. Other jobs with bright futures are those of restaurant manager and hotel housekeeper.

Hotel and Motel Industry

The hotel and motel industry is a major part of hospitality and recreation. Over 3 million hotel and motel rooms serve business and leisure travelers. Most of these are found in large cities such as New York, Boston, Atlanta, Chicago, and San Francisco. About 45 percent of all people who stay in hotels and motels travel for recreation. About 36 percent travel on business. And about 16 percent travel to visit friends and family.

People stay at many different hotels and motels:

- Independent roadside motels
- Budget motels
- Chain motels or hotels
- Luxury hotels
- Convention centers
- Resorts
- Bed and breakfast inns

From seasonal ski resort to beachside hotel, country inn to downtown high rise, each type caters to the needs of certain types of travelers. They differ in cost, services, and atmosphere.

The large variety of hotels allows for flexibility within the industry. Hotels specialize in order to attract specific types of customers, whether business travelers, families, or singles.

Hotels at resort or vacation spots offer special programs to enjoy the area. They may have a ski instructor or golf teacher on the staff. Or they may provide tours of a nearby attraction.

In the past, hotels got business mainly on the basis of location. As more and more hotels have been built, though, competition has grown. To get an edge, hotels and motels are beginning to offer more services. Hotels provide luxury suites, cable TV, rides to the airport, health clubs, shopping, and a choice of restaurants. Travelers have come to expect more from a hotel or motel than simply a comfortable room.

A major trend in the hotel and motel industry is the expansion of franchises, or chains. Half of the 3 million hotel and motel rooms in the United States are controlled by the 25 major hotel chains. The chains have grown tremendously in recent years.

A big reason for the popularity of the chains is that customers know what to expect. All hotels in a chain usually offer the same kinds of rooms and services. As a result, the rooms are familiar to travelers no matter what city they visit. Travelers like having something they can count on.

The rise of chains is important to workers as well. Chains may offer better salaries than independent hotels. They also provide more job opportunities. Workers willing to move to another city or state may find more chances for advancement open to them.

Independent hotels offer a different benefit. They are often smaller than a chain hotel. As a result, a worker may be called on to do a greater variety of jobs.

The hotel and motel industry can expect steady growth through the year 2000. Analysts predict that the lodging industry will expand by 1.0 to 1.5 percent each year. This will mean 11,000 to 16,500 new jobs per year.

Food Service

Restaurant chains, especially those serving fast food, have changed the food service industry within the United States. Food sales at chain restaurants are increasing at least 15 percent every year. This is a result of the changing American way of life. Family members have separate schedules from one another and are constantly on the move. More mothers now work, and teenagers are getting their own meals. Adults make plans for special events after work. They want good food served quickly and at reasonable prices.

Today the average person eats out three to four times a week. Americans spend over $150 billion dollars a year eating out. Of every dollar spent by an American on food, 40 cents is spent in restaurants.

Food service is one of the fastest-growing industries in the country today. Jobs are expected to grow nearly three times as fast as in the overall work force. Food service jobs in government food and housing programs will grow more than twice as fast as other jobs in the industry.

The restaurant industry includes a variety of restaurants: fast-food restaurants and small coffee shops, hotel restaurants, and ethnic and gourmet restaurants are just some. Institutions such as colleges and universities or retirement homes also employ food-service workers.

A food-service job that will offer excellent opportunities in the future is chef. About 100,000 chef jobs open every year to high school graduates who qualify. Another common career is waiter or waitress.

Fitness and Recreation

Recreation is a big part of our lives today. Fitness centers are cropping up in city business districts, malls, and at workplaces. People are spending more of their free time at leisure activities they enjoy—ball games, golf, swimming, and more.

Fitness and recreation workers help people enjoy themselves in many different settings:

- Resorts, hotels, and vacation spots
- Playgrounds, parks, and beaches
- Community pools and recreation centers
- Youth and senior citizens centers
- Exercise clubs and golf courses
- Sports stadiums

A number of trends combine to increase the demand for fitness and recreation workers. Americans have more leisure time today than ever before. They are also living longer. As a result, different kinds of recreation are needed to fit all ages and physical abilities.

Another reason for the boom in fitness is the growth in information. Americans are better aware of their health and nutrition than they were in the past. They are eating more sensibly and exercising regularly.

Even businesses are realizing the importance of healthy employees. More private companies now offer on-site exercise facilities.

As a result of these trends, Americans will spend over $5 billion to join the more than 11,000 exercise and fitness clubs in our country. New health clubs are springing up every day. For these reasons, workers in fitness and recreation will be needed in large numbers.

Chapter 1
Hotel and Motel Desk Clerk

Desk clerks are among the first workers that guests at a hotel or motel meet. They deal constantly with the public and should set the tone for friendliness and hospitality.

Education, Training, and Salary

Most hotels require that a desk clerk have a high school education. Good typing, bookkeeping, and office machine skills can be very helpful for the job.

Desk clerks usually start out as bellhops, switchboard operators, or key clerks, who give out room keys. This helps them learn about the workings of the hotel. With experience and training, these workers can move up to be desk clerks.

Desk clerks in large cities earn from $12,000 to $18,000 a year. If they belong to a labor union, there may be rules about salary and pay increases. Desk clerks usually receive good benefits, such as insurance and retirement plans. They also may receive free meals during work hours.

Hotels and motels are open twenty-four hours a day, seven days a week. Desk clerks work a day or night shift. They may have to work weekends and holidays or six days a week. If they have to work odd hours, clerks may receive extra pay.

Job Description

Desk clerks' jobs depend on the size of the hotel or motel. In smaller motels and hotels, they do many different jobs.

Desk clerks take guests' reservations, check in guests when they arrive, assign them a room, and give them a key. Clerks tell guests any important information they might need to know about the hotel services, special events, or the town in which they are staying. And desk clerks supervise housekeeping and bellhop staffs.

In very large hotels, separate clerks may do each job. Key clerks give out and receive room keys. Rack clerks know which rooms are filled and which are available, and tell the housekeepers what rooms need to be cleaned. Reservations clerks reserve rooms ahead of time by phone or mail. They let the room clerk know when guests will be checking in and out and how many there will be. Mail clerks handle guests' mail or telegrams. Information clerks give directions and facts about the area.

Desk clerks need to know about all the services that the hotel or motel offers. That way they can answer guests' questions quickly and correctly. Guests are often travelers from another part of the country. Unfamiliar with the area where the hotel is, they may ask directions or request the name of a good restaurant. Clerks who can give this information help the guest feel welcome.

Many hotel desk clerks wear uniforms when they are on duty. These uniforms are provided by the hotel. Clerks are responsible for keeping them clean and in good condition.

16

Desk clerks must be friendly and helpful to each guest. And they must be able to get along easily with people and handle any problems that

---

Talking About the Job

More towels for Room 1202. Car for Room 655. Dinner reservations for Room 1412.

As usual, I'm juggling phone calls from guests here at the Plaza Star Resort Hotel. I'm Andre Santell and I have been a desk clerk here for three years. I like the work because it's always busy. I never sit around with nothing to do.

I switch phone calls to the right departments, send towels to housekeeping, and refer dinner reservations to the restaurant. I like the idea of balancing different responsibilities, since I oversee the other employees up front.

Since ours is a pretty large hotel, we have a lot of people behind the desk. Phones are constantly ringing, and we have to move out of each other's way when there is a big check-in rush.

We are a resort hotel, which means that we offer many activities such as swimming, horseback riding, tennis, and night-club shows. I keep track of what activities are planned so that I can tell guests about them.

I work with a computer that tells me the available rooms and how many beds are in each. When people call in or mail in reservations, we put the information in the computer so we always know how many openings we have.

Someday, I hope to work up to a job as hotel manager. These days I'm taking a night class in hotel management at Oakwood Junior College in town. The class meets on Tuesdays and Thursdays. My salary helps me pay for the classes, and I'm still able to save some.

I like working at a resort hotel because I can use the facilities when I'm off duty. I can swim, play racquetball, and use the weight room when it's not a busy time for guests. Those are great benefits to me, so I guess I'd say hotel desk clerk is a great job.

The desk clerk gives customers friendly, helpful service to convince them to return to the hotel.

may come up. Since motel and hotel desk clerks work in front, guests usually come to them first with questions or complaints. Patience is often needed in dealing with guests who have special demands. If the problem cannot be solved quickly and easily, clerks may have to bring in the manager.

Hotel and motel desk clerks work on their feet a lot, and they may do a lot of walking from one area to another. But they work in neat, clean surroundings—sometimes very luxurious ones.

Outlook for Jobs

An experienced desk clerk who works hard and shows management that he or she is dependable may be promoted.

This promotion may be to assistant manager of a hotel. In some hotels, a clerk may move up to front office manager. These jobs mean higher pay and more responsibility.

Many colleges and junior colleges offer classes in hotel and motel management. These classes are helpful for hotel workers who wish to advance their careers within the field.

Some hotels offer financial aid to help young people take college courses.

The hotel and motel industry is expected to grow through the year 2000. This means more workers will be needed to provide the many important services and conveniences guests expect during their stays.

For more information on hotel and motel desk clerks, write to:

American Hotel and Motel Association
1201 New York Avenue, NW
Washington, DC 20005
(202) 289–3100

Council on Hotel, Restaurant, and Institutional Education
311 First Street, NW
Washington, DC 20001
(202) 628–0038

Hotel Employees and Restaurant Employees International Union
1219 Twenty-eighth Street, NW
Washington, DC 20007
(202) 393–4373

Chapter 2
Outdoor Guide

Working in the great outdoors—it's some people's idea of the perfect job. Outdoor guides are usually expert at hunting and fishing and have experience in hiking and camping. Often self-taught, they are enthusiastic teachers about nature and the art of survival.

Education, Training, and Salary

There is no education requirement for outdoor guides. Guides often need permits or licenses to work as hunting or fishing guides. They may need to pass a test to qualify to drive a boat. They must know the terrain where they will work. They should understand and respect the environment of the area. Guides also need to know how to survive outdoors under any circumstances.

The average yearly salary for outdoor guides is $10,500. Because guides work on their own, they charge what they think is fair for each trip. Some guides work for groups such as the Audubon Society. Guides who become park rangers work for the federal government.

Job Description

Most outdoor guides are in business for themselves, so they must offer solid, dependable service. They sign up customers to go on fishing, hunting, canoeing, backpacking, photographic, or nature-study trips.

Some groups hire an outdoor guide for a three-day canoe ride down a local river. Another group might ask the guide to supervise a three-week backpacking trip across Alaska. Or a group might want to study plants and flowers in a national park for a few hours.

Guides help customers choose the equipment they will need for their particular trip. This includes the type of clothing, camping supplies, and food. Guides are also in charge of the group's transportation.

Outdoor guides need many skills. They plan, organize, lead, drive, cook, and give first aid for their groups.

Following state laws on hunting and fishing is an important part of the guide's job. Each state has its own laws. Guides must make sure that their groups obey these laws and leave the area the way they found it.

Guides must be well trained in wilderness survival and always ready for the unexpected. What could happen to a group on a two-day outdoor trip? Here are a few possibilities:
- The group could be attacked by an unfriendly animal, such as a bear or coyote.
- A member of the group could get an injury such as a sprained ankle.
- Routes might be blocked because of a heavy snowfall or flooding.
- A group member could fall out of a canoe.
- The group members could quarrel among themselves or disregard the guide's advice.

Park rangers teach the public by conducting tours of natural and historical areas.

Outdoor guides may work outdoors year round. Bad weather does not stop them or their groups from setting out on their trips.

Physical strength is another requirement for guides. They might have to strap on large backpacks or portage. This means carrying canoes over land between bodies of water.

Outlook for Jobs

The job outlook for outdoor guides differs for each area of the country. For example, an outdoor guide who takes groups on white-water raft trips in Colorado might get more groups than a guide in another state.

Guides who work alone must create business. Outdoor guides who are self-starters will get more customers than those who sit back and wait for customers to come to them. Guides may need to advertise their services in outdoor sporting magazines, in newspapers, or by sending out pamphlets or brochures.

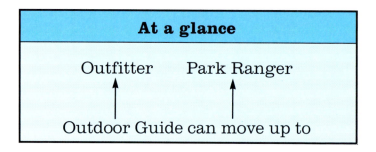

At a glance
Outfitter   Park Ranger ↑   ↑ | | Outdoor Guide can move up to

Job opportunities generally look good for guides. The amount of business a guide gets, though, depends on the reputation he or she builds. If one satisfied group tells another about "this terrific guide," that guide will be hired more often. If a dissatisfied group spreads the word about a guide, that guide is likely to get less work.

Some outdoor guides choose to become outfitters. An outfitter runs a business that "outfits" people who will go on outdoor trips or join in nature activities. The outfitter provides clothes and equipment and also gives advice about the kind of activity the customer will be doing.

Outdoor guides might also become park rangers. Rangers work for the government, helping to protect national parks and forests.

High school graduates can train to become park rangers. They must work and get experience in conservation and park operations. It is helpful to take some college courses while they train.

Park rangers are trained to protect people and natural resources such as plants and flowers. Rangers help campers build safe campsites, deal with animals, and prevent harm to the environment.

At national parks and historic places, rangers teach visitors by showing movies, speaking to groups, and answering questions about the places of interest.

Park rangers also enforce the law. They are like wilderness police officers. They see that rules are followed and that those breaking the rules pay a fine or are arrested.

For more information on outdoor guides or park rangers, write to:

American Forestry Association
1516 P Street, NW
Washington, DC 20005
(202) 667–3300

American Guides Association
Road 94B
Woodland, CA 95695

National Recreation and Park Association
3101 Park Center Drive
Alexandria, VA 22302

Chapter 3
Hotel Cook or Chef and Baker

Hotel Cook or Chef

Hotel restaurants offer delicious meals that appeal to travelers. The food and service should keep them coming back to the hotel. Preparing those tasty meals is the job of the cook or chef.

Education, Training, and Salary A high school education is required for cooks and chefs. Cooks train on the job, but they can get formal instruction, too. The armed forces offer cook's training, as do vocational and technical schools.

Cooks might begin as dishwashers or kitchen helpers and work their way up.

Cooks start at about $4.75 to $6.00 an hour. Chefs at small restaurants earn from $20,000 to $35,000 a year. The larger the restaurant, the higher the pay. Very well known chefs can earn more than $80,000 a year. Cooks and chefs usually receive benefits such as medical insurance, paid vacations, and holidays.

Job Description As the kitchen supervisor, the chef oversees all the other cooks in the kitchen. He or she plans the menu, decides how much food is served and how it is arranged, and orders the supplies.

27

In large kitchens, many cooks and chefs may work, each on a special kind of cooking. These include fry cook, pastry chef, salad chef, soup cook, and others. All work under a main chef.

Cooks do demanding work. They stand for long periods of time. They also lift many heavy pots and other equipment. They often work nights, weekends, and holidays.

Outlook for Jobs   Cooks may advance in their careers by being promoted and being given more responsibility and higher pay. They can also move up by moving to other restaurants.

Cooks who want to become chefs must get several years of kitchen experience. Advanced cooking classes are also helpful.

Some cooks decide to go into business for themselves. They buy a restaurant or start a catering service, preparing and serving foods for groups. Owning a business takes more than good cooking skills. The cook needs money and business knowledge. Other cooks teach, either in high school or adult education classes.

The future looks excellent for cooks and chefs, with thousands of jobs opening. As more restaurants open, more cooks and chefs will be needed.

Baker

Education, Training, and Salary   A high school education is required for most baker jobs. Many bakers train on the job.

Bakers average $16,000 to $18,500 a year. Experienced bakers can earn up to $35,000. Some pastry chefs earn more than $50,000.

Talking About the Job

"This is the best meal I have ever had." These words are music to a cook's ears. They make all the hours of standing on my feet, chopping, mixing, and simmering worthwhile.

I ought to know. I'm Michael Washington, and I am a kitchen helper in a large hotel restaurant. You can probably guess what attracted me to this line of work. That's right, I love food.

When I graduated from high school last year, I applied to a restaurant in the area. The only experience I had was cooking for my family. But it turned out that it was a pretty good place to start. It gave me a feel for working with food, and I learned a lot of things just from using common sense.

I really learn a lot watching the cooks who have been here for years. They know the tricks and the shortcuts. Most important, they know how to fix a dish that has gone wrong.

Once, when a soup was too salty, I saw a chef put in a peeled raw potato. He left it in for a while, then took it out and threw it away. You know what happened? The potato had soaked up a lot of the salt, and the soup tasted better.

The chef gives me certain jobs to do each day. I might chop up vegetables for soup or measure out ingredients for a recipe to save the chef time.

I have two choices when I'm ready to move up to a higher job. I can either apply to a smaller restaurant as a cook or train to be a chef. It's a decision I can put off for a while because I'm doing well here. And I know that while I'm working here I'm always learning.

I'm glad I enjoy my job. I don't even mind working longer hours or on weekends and holidays. As long as I'm in the kitchen, I'm happy.

Job Description   The person responsible for the delicious aroma of fresh breads, pies, and other baked goods is the baker. Like the cooks and other kitchen workers, the baker is supervised by the chef.

29

A baker prepares bread and other baked goods in restaurants and in the kitchens of institutions.

Bakers might work for large hotels or small neighborhood doughnut shops. Sometimes assistants help bakers by preparing the basic dough to be used in many different recipes. Or they might check the times and temperatures needed for baked goods.

Bakers must know how to use the many different machines that help make baked goods in large amounts. They use blending machines, dividing machines, and dough molders, among others.

Outlook for Jobs　　Bakers in industrial baking operations can move up to supervisory positions, overseeing the other workers. These production bakers and supervisors usually follow an advancement plan set by their company.

If production bakers get more training and develop more advanced skills, they may move into retail, restaurant, or hotel baking positions.

Starting in smaller restaurants and moving to larger ones is a good way to get experience.

With more machines doing the work in large bakeries, bakers may find fewer jobs there in the future. But in small bakeries, where much of the work is still done by hand, jobs will always be open.

The outlook is also excellent for pastry chefs in fine restaurants. Special training in cooking schools can prepare young people for this career.

For more information on cooks, chefs, or bakers, write to:

American Bakers Association
1111 Fourteenth Street, NW
Washington, DC 20005
(202) 296–5800

American Culinary Federation
P. O. Box 3466
St. Augustine, FL 32084
(904) 824–4468
(202) 289–3100

**Hotel Employees and Restaurant Employees
    International Union**
1219 Twenty-eighth Street, NW
Washington, DC 20007
(202) 393–4373

National Restaurant Association
311 First Street, NW
Washington, DC 20001
(202) 638–6100

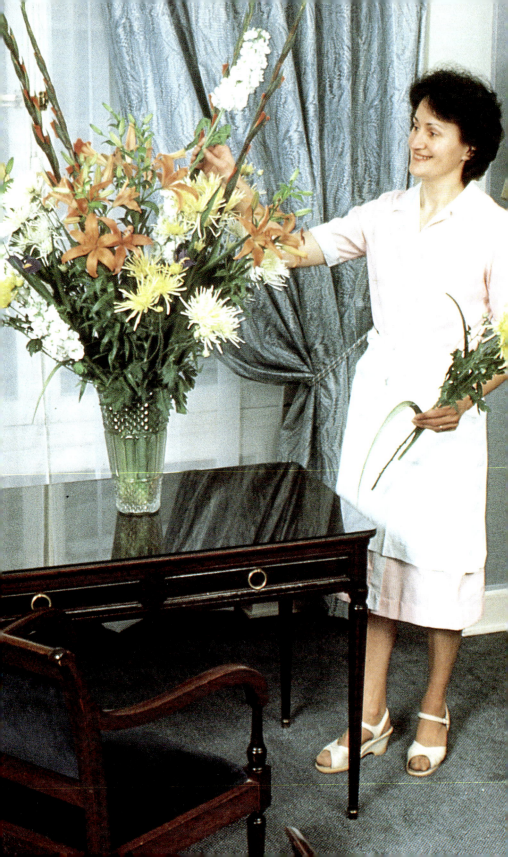

Chapter 4
Hotel Housekeeper

Many services keep hotel customers coming back to the same place. One of the most noticeable is housekeeping. Freshly made beds and plenty of clean towels can make a hotel stand out in the minds of its guests. The housekeeping staff performs this important job.

Education, Training, and Salary

Most employers prefer hiring workers with a high school education. Experience in cleaning is helpful. Most hotels provide on-the-job training.

Hotel housekeepers can average hourly salaries of $3.35 to $6.00. Experienced workers can earn yearly salaries of $12,000 or more. Beginning executive housekeepers in large hotels can earn $12,000 to $15,000 yearly.

Job Description

Some housekeepers run the laundry, which provides clean towels and bed linens for guests. They also clean hotel employees' uniforms.

Others are responsible only for guests' rooms. They wheel carts stocked with cleaning supplies to rooms. Room housekeepers change the beds, empty wastebaskets and ashtrays, dust and polish furniture, vacuum carpets, make sure lights work, clean windows and bathrooms, and remove all trash and soiled linens from rooms.

A guest who checked out may have accidentally left something behind. The housekeeper's job is to bring it to the hotel's office, so the guest can be notified.

Some housekeepers work behind the scenes. They repair torn curtains or linens. They may also have duties to maintain machines.

Hallways and stairs also must be kept clean and neat. Housekeepers in large hotels may have miles of hallways to vacuum each day. Housekeepers must maintain every public area of the hotel as well.

Housekeeping supervisors often work in larger hotels, organizing workers on each floor. In smaller hotels, one or two housekeepers might have the responsibility of cleaning all areas. They may also clean towels, linens, and uniforms in the laundry.

Hotels and motels are usually attractive places to work. Since hotels are open twenty-four hours, the work may go beyond a regular eight-hour day. In large hotels, the housekeeping staff is split into shifts so that some workers are always on duty. And of course, hotels are open holidays and weekends—every day of the year.

Housekeeping is hard work. Newer hotels and motels may provide powerful, up-to-date equipment that makes chores easier. But all housekeepers must do very physical work. They need to bend, stoop, reach, and clean. While the equipment helps them do their jobs, it can be heavy to move.

Being clean and neat is a big part of housekeeping work. A neatly made bed and well-kept room appeals to guests. Housekeepers also need to pay attention to details. They must look in every corner to find spots that need cleaning.

Some housekeepers work in institutions such as colleges and hospitals. They must be careful and clean as well—they are cleaning the place where someone lives.

Outlook for Jobs

Housekeepers with experience and training can move up to be executive housekeepers. If they work for a hotel chain, they may have the opportunity to transfer to other hotel locations within the chain.

Executive housekeepers may be in charge of the entire housekeeping staff—sometimes hundreds of workers. They order supplies and make up budgets for the housekeeping department.

An executive housekeeper assigns a schedule to the housekeepers on the staff.

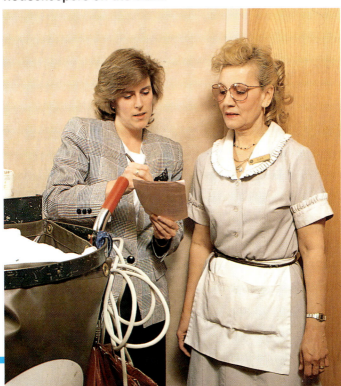

Executive housekeepers keep track of everything that comes into and goes out of the housekeeping supply room. They need good organizational skills and good record-keeping abilities. By keeping track of supplies, they make sure that the housekeeping money is used wisely.

They train new staff and are in charge of assigning jobs to workers. They often have attended college, with a major in home economics or hotel services. Executive housekeepers must be able to manage people fairly and make sure they are performing their jobs well. Like all managers, they must explain the hotel's policies to workers.

Hotel executive housekeepers who receive specialized training in their field may join the National Executive Housekeepers Association. An executive housekeeper must take at least seventy-seven hours of training to become a member.

The future outlook for hotel housekeepers is excellent. About 18,000 housekeepers and housekeeper's assistants worked in hotels by the late 1980s. More openings are expected for these positions in the 1990s, with new hotels and motels being built.

New hotels and motels will be needed to handle the expected increase in business and vacation travelers. Many more foreign travelers will be likely to visit the United States as we head toward the year 2000 as well. The new hotels and motels will require housekeeping help, and so will existing ones. Hotel and motel managers are always looking for hardworking people to join their housekeeping staffs.

Housekeeping jobs will also open at college and university dormitories, hospitals, and state institutions. Seasonal housekeeping jobs, such as those at summer vacation resorts and at winter ski resorts, will always be available.

For more information on hotel housekeepers, write to:

American Hotel and Motel Association
1201 New York Avenue, NW
Washington, DC 20005
(202) 289–3100

Council on Hotel, Restaurant and Institutional Education
311 First Street, NW
Washington, DC 20001
(202) 628–0038

Interested people should also apply directly to hotels, motels, resorts, or institutions that may need housekeeping help. Check newspaper classified ads and your state employment office for job opportunities.

Chapter 5
Waiter or Waitress and Host or Hostess

Waiter or Waitress

When customers order a meal in a restaurant, they want it served as soon as possible and at the right temperature. The person responsible for delivering the meal is the waiter or waitress.

Education, Training, and Salary

ployers prefer that a waiter or waitress have a high school education. Most of these workers train on the job. In finer restaurants, they often need more training and experience. They may start busing tables and work their way up.

Waiters and waitresses average $4.30 an hour plus tips. How much can be earned from tips varies with the kind of restaurant. It also depends on the quality of service the worker provides. Benefits include medical insurance, paid vacations, and some meals.

Job Description

After the customers are seated, waiters or waitresses begin work. They must know about the dishes on the menu and how they are prepared. That way they can answer any questions customers ask about the food.

Good service includes remembering who ordered what. People appreciate having their meal set down in front of them without a waiter calling out, "Who had the roast duck?"

Good waiters and waitresses keep checking back with the table during the meal to see if a customer needs hot coffee, or if the meal is not satisfactory. After the meal, they offer dessert.

When guests have finished, the waiter or waitress adds up the check and presents it.

In small restaurants, waiters and waitresses do the work performed by many workers in a larger restaurant. They may show people to tables, which hostesses would normally do. They might refill water glasses; clean tables; replace soiled tablecloths, napkins, and silverware; or fill sugar, pepper, and salt containers. These jobs are usually done by busboys. Or they might work the cash register.

Waiters and waitresses work day or evening shifts, and many holidays and weekends. Many waiters and waitresses work part time.

Outlook for Jobs   The future for waiters and waitresses looks excellent. Most openings are in lower-priced restaurants. In higher-priced restaurants, there is a lot of competition for jobs.

Host or Hostess

The host or hostess is the first person that guests meet in the restaurant. So he or she can make an important first impression.

Education, Training, and Salary   Most restaurants prefer hosts and hostesses to have a high school education. Hosts and hostesses train on the job. It can help to have a background as a waiter or waitress.

Talking About the Job

Sometimes I dream about ham and swiss on rye, hold the mayo, fries on the side. I write so many sandwich orders during my shift that I could do it with my eyes closed!

I'm Georgia Martine and I work at The Village Diner. I've been a waitress here for a long time. I've liked it here with all the friends I've made over the years. Liz and Janie and I have been here for a total of twelve years. We wouldn't work anywhere else.

But you have to like being on your feet. I bought a pair of comfortable sneakers, and my feet really thank me. I have to replace my shoes pretty often. They wear out fast.

Our diner serves a big lunch crowd, mostly from the businesses and factories in the neighborhood. We have a lot of regulars who come in every week, and it's good to see the familiar faces. I know it's Thursday when Joe and Stan walk through the door.

The owner of the restaurant greets people when they come in and seats them at tables. Then my job begins. I have an area called a station, which is where I work. When people are seated at my station, I go into action.

I get paid an hourly wage plus tips. The tips make up most of my earnings. I've been able to save quite a bit each month by putting away money in the bank. And I know that the nicer I am to customers, the better the chance that I'll get a good tip.

I like people, so this job is good for me. I like to talk with the customers I know and catch up on what's been happening. And it's nice to welcome new customers and serve them well. It's a good feeling to think that I'm one of the reasons they come back.

Hosts and hostesses average $3.75 to $7.00 an hour. They may earn more than $15,000 a year. They sometimes receive tips. Benefits may include medical insurance, paid holidays, vacations, and retirement plans. Hosts and hostesses also get free meals during working hours.

41

The restaurant staff, headed by the host, makes customers feel welcome.

Job Description   Hosts and hostesses greet customers and show them to their tables. They must make sure the table is acceptable, or check to see if something special, like a high chair, is needed. On a busy night, they must also figure out how long a customer must wait for a table.

Hosts or hostesses may take phone reservations for lunch or dinner. They must make sure the number of reservations is not greater than the number of available tables. They also keep track of people arriving and leaving to help the staff know when tables must be cleaned and set for new guests.

Hosts and hostesses often work as cashiers also, taking money and making change at the cash register. If the restaurant has a candy and gum counter, the host or hostess may be in charge of it.

The restaurant manager may require the host or hostess to total up the money at the end of the shift. So he or she must be good at math to keep track of the accounting duties.

Hosts and hostesses must be polite and courteous to all guests and help out wherever needed. It is often a busy job, especially at peak times such as Saturday night dinner.

Outlook for Jobs   Hosts and hostesses can move up by transferring to larger restaurants. With experience and business knowledge, they may become restaurant managers.

Most restaurants have only one or two host or hostess shifts available. As a result, there is competition for these jobs. Openings occur when hosts and hostesses move to other restaurants or retire.

For more information on waiters, waitresses, hosts, or hostesses, write to:

Hotel Employees and Restaurant Employees International Union
1219 Twenty-eighth Street, NW
Washington, DC 20007
(202) 393–4373

National Restaurant Association
311 First Street, NW
Washington, DC 20001
(202) 638–6100

Interested people should also apply directly to restaurants.

Chapter 6
Entertainment or Social Director and Recreation Worker

Entertainment or Social Director

Leisure time is important to people. They want to join in activities that interest them and socialize with others. They often look to trained recreation workers to lead them in these activities.

Education, Training, and Salary   A high school education is needed to work as an entertainment or social director. Courses in physical education, music, dance, and art are helpful.

Training may differ from place to place. Some entertainment or social directors are trained on the job. Others are hired with experience. A good way to gain experience is to work summers as a recreation leader or camp counselor.

Entertainment or social directors usually start out around $14,000 to $16,000 a year. Salaries depend on the level of the job, the place, and whether the work is part-time or full-time.

Entertainment or social directors at hotels and resorts often get meals while they are on duty. They may also receive free rooms and laundry service. Full-time workers may get other benefits, such as vacations, sick leave, medical insurance, and retirement benefits.

45

Job Description   Entertainment or social directors work in many different places. Summer camps, resorts, hotels, senior citizens centers, day-care centers, and correctional institutions are some examples.

Entertainment or social directors provide many services for people of all ages. They lead classes in arts and crafts. They teach music. Sometimes they arrange dances and other social gatherings. With their help, people often can meet others with whom they share interests.

At senior citizens centers, social directors may be especially important in getting older people together. Some elderly people are lonely. Social activities are an important way for senior citizens to keep in touch with others.

Entertainment or social directors often organize field trips to interesting places. These might be a ballet, museum, play, concert, or zoo.

Many entertainment or social directors lead simple exercise classes for groups. The director must make sure that the level of exercise is right for the age and physical abilities of the group.

Resort hotels often employ entertainment or social directors. They plan daytime or evening social activities for their guests. These may include a staff talent show on Tuesday, a Hawaiian luau on Wednesday, and an "Oldies" dance on Friday.

Social directors at hotels and resorts may also organize activities for the children or guests. They must be trained to keep children of all ages entertained and happy.

Entertainment or social directors must be friendly and outgoing. It's important for social

Camp counselors are teachers as well. Here, a counselor gives archery lessons to a group of children.

directors to make shy people more comfortable in the group. They should enjoy meeting people and making new friends.

Creativity and a good imagination are important, too. After all, social directors must come up with new and interesting activities. And they must be physically fit and able to lead exercises and take groups on outings.

Outlook for Jobs   An entertainment or social director can be promoted to be assistant manager of a resort or hotel.

The future looks good for young people who want to become entertainment or social directors. Vacationers will always look for trained workers to lead them in activities.

The number of senior citizens is on the rise. As more retirement homes are being built, the number of these jobs will increase.

Recreation Worker

Education, Training, and Salary

Recreation workers must have a high school education. Many train while they work. Specialized recreation workers often require further training in the areas in which they will teach. Training in physical education and personal fitness is necessary for teaching sports and exercise to children and adults.

Recreation workers' salaries vary from place to place. They usually earn about $500 a week. The work may be seasonal.

Job Description

Some recreation workers are employed by city recreation departments or park districts. They may help a recreation director plan educational programs in which they teach crafts, a language, juggling, or storytelling. Or they might plan physical activities such as gymnastics, ballet, or tennis.

Outlook for Jobs

With several years' experience, a recreation worker can move up to be assistant to the recreation director or even to the job of recreation director itself.

With more leisure time, higher incomes, longer life expectancies, and earlier retirement for workers, recreation workers will be in demand through the year 2000.

Youth sports programs at camps, city recreation departments, and park districts will need workers to fill jobs. And with more children getting involved in organized sports, more programs are being set up.

Government recreation programs do not hire as many workers in slow economic times.

48

Summer Jobs in Recreation

Summer camps often hire young people to teach swimming or arts and crafts, or to lead guitar sing-alongs around a campfire. These workers often receive room, meals, and use of the facilities as part of their payment.

Camp counselors must be able to set up a tent, hike, understand nature, swim and teach others to swim, and work with groups. To teach swimming or diving, they must be trained in Red Cross Lifesaving. And they must know first aid and CPR, or cardiopulmonary resuscitation.

Summer jobs in parks and recreation usually pay from the minimum wage up to about $5.00 an hour.

A summer job as an unpaid volunteer or as a part-time paid worker is valuable experience for full-time work in recreation.

For more information on entertainment or social directors and recreation workers, write to:

American Camping Association
5000 State Road, 67 North
Martinsville, IN 46151
(317) 342–8456

Council on Hotel, Restaurant and Institutional Education
311 First Street, NW
Washington, DC 20001
(202) 628–0038

Interested young people should also apply directly to places that may hire these workers.

Chapter 7
Fitness Instructor and Sports Director

Today, people are concerned with being in shape. They are exercising more, eating healthier foods, and paying better attention to their health.

Fitness instructors and sports directors help others keep fit. These workers are found in health clubs, gyms, sports training centers, and schools. Some work in fitness or exercise centers that businesses create for their workers.

Fitness Instructor

Education, Training, and Salary   A high school education is required for a job as a fitness instructor. It is helpful to understand sports injuries—how they happen, how to prevent them, and how to help them heal. Many hospitals and colleges offer courses.

Young people interested in this work should take classes in CPR and first aid. They should learn as much as possible about how the body works. Understanding the body and its muscles and joints and knowing the importance of good nutrition are important to making a good fitness program.

Fitness instructors usually earn about $4.00 to $15.00 an hour.

Job Description　　Fitness instructors lead people in aerobics, weight training, calisthenics, running, and race walking. Many instructors specialize in one area, such as body building.

Fitness instructors must be physically fit. Many take classes in fitness and become certified to teach at centers. They also need to be good communicators so they can teach others how to work out. And they need to be patient when someone does not learn right away how to do an exercise.

Instructors may teach sports at country clubs, golf courses, or tennis centers. They are hired by the centers for their members or guests. Often members pay an hourly rate to sign up for these classes.

Teaching dance is another area for fitness instructors. These teachers must know the steps to a variety of dances.

Since most people exercise or look for fitness-related activities after work, in evenings, or on weekends, instructors usually are most in demand during these times.

Sports Director

Education, Training, and Salary　　Sports directors often must take college courses in sports medicine, biology, and other subjects that teach them about the human body. They must know a great deal about sports and how to run a well-rounded sports program. Young people may get training by starting out as an assistant to a sports director.

Sports directors earn $20,000 or more a year.

A personal exercise trainer teaches health club members how to safely use a weight machine.

Job Description   Sports directors may work at a junior high or high school, heading up the athletics department. They organize the school's athletics program, set the rules, and oversee all sports activities. They may be in charge of equipment, supplies, and setting up practice and playing facilities. Sports directors also hire the coaches.

Some sports directors work for colleges. They also hire coaches, looking for people with advanced training and background in a particular sport.

53

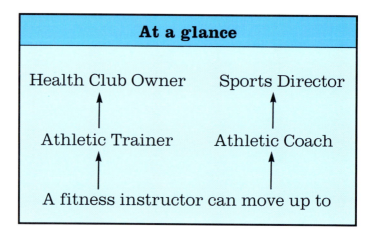

At a glance

Health Club Owner   Sports Director

↑   ↑

Athletic Trainer   Athletic Coach

↑   ↑

A fitness instructor can move up to

Outlook for Jobs   The future looks good for jobs in the fitness and athletics field. The growing awareness of fitness is responsible for creating more health clubs, fitness centers, and gyms, so staff is always needed. And company-run exercise centers need staff to plan programs for their employees.

Schools look for capable people to join their athletic departments and help train athletes. These jobs are limited. They generally become open only when a worker moves to another job or retires.

Getting experience as a fitness instructor is a good background for a person who wants to become a sports director or take another supervisory position in the sports and fitness field.

Some instructors start by working at an exercise center. Then they decide to open their own fitness and training centers. Often, customers will move with them to the new location.

For more information on fitness instructors or sports directors, write to:

Association for Fitness in Business
965 Hope Street
Stamford, CT 06907
(203) 359–2188

Association of Physical Fitness Centers
600 Jefferson Street
Rockville, MD 20852
(301) 424–7744

National Athletic Trainers Association
1001 East 4th Street, Box 1865
Greenville, NC 27858
(919) 752–1725

National High School Athletic Coaches Association
P.O. Box 1808
Ocala, FL 32678
(904) 622–3660

Chapter 8
Groundskeeper and Stadium Worker

Keeping the grounds of a sports stadium, golf course, country club, racetrack, or other outdoor area in good shape takes year-round maintenance. Groundskeepers and other maintenance workers are the ones who take care of these facilities.

Education, Training, and Salary

Groundskeepers and stadium workers should have a high school education. Civil service exams may be required for jobs working in stadiums owned by a city. (Civil service exams are discussed on page 84.)

Many landscaping companies hire young people to help with grounds during the summer. This is good training for a future in groundskeeping. Most training is done on the job for stadium workers.

Stadium workers and groundskeepers who belong to labor unions can earn $11,000 to $17,000 a year. When they move up to be supervisors, they can earn at least $23,000 a year. Groundskeepers with experience can earn up to $19,000 a year.

Stadium concessions workers may work on a straight commission basis. This means they earn money based on how much food they sell. Ticket takers and ushers may earn $4.50 to $8.00 an hour. Benefits for full-time workers can be very good, with a retirement plan, medical insurance, overtime pay, and paid vacations and holidays. Sometimes food service workers receive free meals.

Job Description

Groundskeepers mow the grass, fertilize lawns, control weeds, trim trees and shrubs, and plant flowers. They can work for public places or for private landscaping services.

In winter, groundskeepers are in charge of putting away picnic tables and benches, shoveling snow, or salting walkways. They make sure that all trash is emptied and that cans are placed around public areas.

At some stadiums groundskeepers are in charge of the artificial turf. They make sure that the turf is safe and not damaged after games. Players can become injured if tears or snags in artificial turf are not repaired.

Many other workers help maintain the area in stadiums. Equipment operators sweep and smooth out baseball diamonds and racetracks. They operate heavy equipment and work with the ground crew to protect the area if it starts to rain.

Ticket takers in stadiums make sure that only paying customers enter the stadiums. Often they must keep track of the number of people who attend an event. Ushers show people to their seats and oversee what goes on in the stands. They handle patrons who are unruly.

Many stadium workers work in food service. Some work for stadium-owned restaurants. Others work at privately owned concession stands,

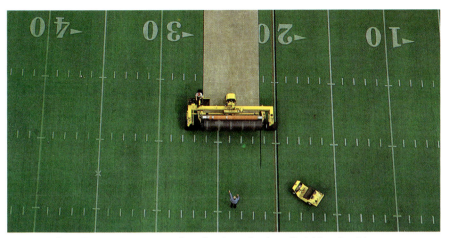
Stadium workers maintain the playing field in the New Orleans Superdome.

which rent space from the stadium. Some concession workers walk through the aisles selling food and drinks to customers.

Groundskeeping and stadium jobs can be seasonal, since some outdoor places close in winter. Many stadium workers work during games and events that take place on evenings and weekends. Custodians may work during the day preparing a stadium for an event. Or they may work cleaning up after events.

Greenskeepers at golf courses maintain the area and oversee other workers. They make up work schedules and assign duties. They also may give public information at the courses.

Outlook for Jobs

The future looks good for stadium workers and groundskeepers. Sporting events, concerts, and other events that take place in stadiums will al-

Talking About the Job

"Peanuts, peanuts, get your fresh roasted peanuts here." That's my line. I'm Jenny List and I sell concessions at Northwest Stadium.

We have a lot of sports events here, which is what got me interested in the job. I'm a baseball fan, so I get to sneak a lot of looks at the game while I walk through the stands. And when everyone cheers, or boos, or jumps up, I spin around to catch the action.

I work here in spring and summer, and I've been doing it for two years now. I like the work, and I like the excitement of the ballpark. The pay can be excellent, especially if you get to move up to the bigger-selling items, hot dogs and soda.

I'm on my feet sometimes up to four hours at a time, so it can be pretty tiring. Like the time the ball game went into extra innings—eight extra innings! I worked the stands for six hours.

I have to move fast sometimes. If a guy waves at me for more peanuts eight rows up, I'll be there. My back is definitely getting strong from hauling that carrier around.

The worst is when someone gives me a twenty-dollar bill for a bag of peanuts. It seems that the person is always sitting about ten seats in from the aisle, so you have to ask the person at the end to pass the change down. But most people don't mind.

The workers who sell a lot are the ice cream sellers in hot weather. They can't keep their coolers filled long enough to walk more than one section!

If you don't mind working some hot days, walking your feet off, and carrying heavy packs, you might like this job as much as I do.

ways be popular. So stadium workers will be needed to keep these places top shape.

Stadium workers who work for the city get promoted by taking and passing civil service exams. There is an exam for each employment level (see page 84). After passing these tests, workers are given a trial period in order to prove that they are skilled enough for their new position. With time and experience, union workers in private stadiums can also move up.

Groundskeepers will be needed in the years to come to maintain private clubs, public outdoor areas, arenas, and other outdoor areas. Private landscaping services are always looking for hardworking young people to replace workers who are leaving or to add to their staff.

For more information on groundskeepers and stadium workers, write to:

International Association of Auditorium Managers
500 North Michigan Avenue
Chicago, IL 60611
(312) 661–1700

Service Employees International Union
1313 L Street, NW
Washington, DC 20005
(202) 898–3200

Young people interested in becoming stadium workers or groundskeepers can apply to golf courses or stadium offices. Those interested in groundskeeping can contact local landscaping companies.

For union jobs, they can contact their local union office for more information.

People interested in concessions work should apply directly to the companies that own concession stands. They can get the phone number or address by calling the stadium office.

Chapter 9
Fast-Food Franchise Worker and Manager

Fast-Food Franchise Worker

Chicken, tacos, hamburgers—fast-food restaurants are more and more popular. People want good, inexpensive food to eat on the run. These restaurants belong to chains, a large group of restaurants that are all the same. About 1.5 million workers serve hamburgers, chicken, fish, and pizza to hungry customers.

Education, Training, and Salary   There is no education requirement for fast-food franchise workers. Fast-food workers are trained on the job. Counter workers should speak clearly to customers and always be polite. It helps to be good at math, too, since counter workers must give customers correct change. Each chain runs its own training program. In that program workers learn everything they need to know about preparing and serving the food the chain offers.

Fast-food franchise workers are usually paid the minimum wage. They get increases with experience. Fast-food franchise workers can earn up to $12,000 a year at some chains. They often are given free meals. Because most workers are part time, they receive no other benefits.

Job Description   Fast-food franchise workers do a variety of jobs. Counter workers take customers' food orders and give them to cooks. They cook french fries, fill drink orders, add side dishes, and make sure that the customers get what they order. The counter worker takes money and makes change.

Most food is prepared by the cook. Some items, like sandwiches, are made ahead of time during busy lunch or dinner hours. Specially heated areas keep the food warm. Each franchise has set cooking methods, whether it is deep-frying, baking, roasting, or broiling.

Each chain also has set amounts for each serving of food. This is one way that chains keep their costs low. Often the cook must weigh the food to make sure it is the set amount. All cooks must follow the practices of their chain.

Cooks may work up to forty-eight hours a week on a full-time basis. Part-time workers usually work twenty to twenty-five hours a week. This works well for students who need to plan their work schedule around school hours. Most employees work some evening and weekend hours.

Those responsible for cleaning up the seating areas are called dining room attendants. They vacuum carpets, mop floors, clean trays, wipe off tables, dispose of trash, clean ashtrays, and fill salt and pepper containers. They also handle trash removal.

Workers should be neat and clean at all times. Health certificates may be required to prove that workers have no illnesses.

Work in a fast-food franchise is not easy. Fast-food workers must prepare and serve food

The fast-food cook must work carefully. Hot grills and hot oil can burn.

quickly. They are on their feet most of the time and do not rest often. The sense of working with others as a team makes the work more enjoyable, though.

Fast-Food Franchise Manager

Education, Training, and Salary   Managers of fast-food restaurants must have a high school education. Courses in business management are also helpful.

Managers often enter company management trainee programs. These may be at the restaurant or at a special site built by the company. There they learn the business side of the chain's activities.

Some companies may require young people to work at other jobs within the restaurant before being promoted to manager. This helps managers know how to direct workers.

Managers can earn from $25,000 to $35,000, depending on the restaurant.

Job Description   Fast-food franchise managers supervise all workers in the restaurant. Managers see that all workers do their jobs and that customers are satisfied. The restaurant often hires a manager for each work shift.

Managers work out schedules for workers so that all shifts are covered. They may do the hiring and the firing of workers. Managers may also recognize hard workers with awards. By providing rewards to good workers, they hope to influence others to work harder, too.

Fast-food chains often create special promotions or events to get more business. Managers are in charge of seeing that the promotion is carried out correctly. Promotions where the franchise gives away game pieces or runs a contest must be kept track of carefully. Managers must be sure that the game or contest is run fairly or there could be legal problems. Other special events such as birthday parties are organized by managers and run by the staff. If this requires special orders, the manager must handle them.

Fast-food franchise managers must keep track of all money coming into the restaurant. They make sure that the cash registers have enough change.

Managers must keep a constant check on food, beverage, and container supplies. They must keep track of delivery schedules and make sure that supplies will last until the next delivery. They tell the owner how business is going.

66

Outlook for Jobs   There is a great deal of turnover in fast-food restaurants. Workers, who are usually part time, are always leaving for other jobs or for school. As a result, there are always openings. This will continue through the year 2000.

Competition is high for manager jobs. Hard workers will be the ones to move up to assistant managers and managers.

For more information on fast-food franchise workers and managers, write to:

International Franchise Association
1350 New York Avenue, NW
Washington, DC 20005

Interested people should also apply directly to fast-food restaurants in their area. Often restaurants will display signs when they are hiring workers. Ads may also appear in the newspaper classified section.

Even if a restaurant is not advertising, people who want to work there should go in and fill out an application. There may not be an immediate opening, but there will probably be one soon.

Chapter 10
Lifeguard and Pool Manager

Lifeguard

Safety is a lifeguard's main concern. When people swim in pools or at beaches, someone must always be on hand in case an accident happens. It takes a trained professional to watch carefully and protect swimmers and to act in an emergency. Lifeguards know the importance of doing their job well. Their swift, trained actions can mean the difference between life and death for someone in trouble.

Education, Training, and Salary A high school education is preferred for lifeguards.

Lifeguards must be well trained to protect people. They must take lifesaving classes and pass swimming and lifesaving tests. Lifeguards must earn a Red Cross Lifesaving certificate to get a job. To keep this certificate, they must take another class every three years. This keeps them up to date on lifesaving and first-aid procedures.

To teach swimming, lifeguards must be over sixteen years old and have a Red Cross Water Safety Instructor certificate. To keep the certificate, an instructor must teach at least one swimming or lifesaving course every two years.

Talking About the Job

I am sitting high above the pool in the warm sun, looking down at the clear blue water and thinking: This is a good job.

But don't get me wrong. This job is no piece of cake. A lot of things can happen, so it's not a relaxing day at the beach.

I'm Carl Zate and I am a lifeguard at Laurelton Community Pool. It's an outdoor pool that's only open from Memorial Day through Labor Day. People from our town join the pool for the summer.

We have lots of little kids who come here, so I have to keep a sharp eye on them. Sometimes they start fooling around with their friends and find themselves in water that's too deep.

It's a good thing I have a loud, strong voice because I have to use it a lot. And believe me, those kids stop what they're doing and look at me. You have to be firm but let them know you're their friend. You want them to trust you and come to you for help if they need it.

This is the best summer job I've ever had. We get a lot of applications from high school kids who want to become lifeguards. They come for interviews, and if the manager thinks they would work out, they take swimming and lifesaving tests.

The manager really checks the kids who are applying really carefully. She asks them lots of questions to see how they think and how they would react in emergencies. She can tell if they wouldn't take the job seriously. She gets a lot of teenagers in here who just want to lounge in the sun. Their interviews are pretty short.

Lifeguards usually start at the minimum wage and get raises as they work longer. Full-time workers receive benefits such as paid vacations and holidays, sick pay, and medical insurance.

Job Description   Lifeguards work at pools and beaches. Some work at public beaches or pools run by the local government. Others work at private swim clubs or hotels and motels.

70

At crowded beaches, lifeguards have special concerns. They may be assigned to rowboats to patrol the deeper waters offshore. They watch for people on rafts who might float too far from the shore or swimmers who might not realize how deep the water is.

At pools, lifeguards must always be on the alert for people in trouble. Young children and others may tire while swimming and need help. Children playing may get too rough and create a danger for themselves and others.

Pool Manager

Education, Training, and Salary   Lifeguards with several years' experience may become pool managers. Some states require a person to get a pool operator's card. This is earned by learning the basics of pool sanitation.

Pool managers can average $6,000 a season at a community pool. Salaries vary at hotels and other places.

Job Description   Pool managers have many important responsibilities. They are in charge of maintaining the pool itself. This means ordering supplies and equipment, cleaning the pool and putting in chemicals, making sure that drains are operating, and checking the water level. Pool managers often hire custodians to do the cleaning around the pool. They must also alert the pool owners or operators if anything needs to be fixed or replaced.

Supervising lifeguards is also a responsibility of managers. They should be able to oversee workers and be a fair boss.

A pool manager is in charge of the pool's cleanliness. Here, the manager teaches an employee about the proper mix of chemicals to keep the pool clean.

A manager's job also may include setting up swimming lessons for children and adults. Some managers organize swimming and diving teams that compete at swim meets.

If the pool has a concession stand, the manager may be in charge of it, or he or she may hire a worker to run it.

Outlook for Jobs With experience, lifeguards can move up to be pool managers or swimming instructors. Instructors teach people of all ages. Most often, they teach young children who may not know swimming basics yet. The children may be afraid of the water and may need a lot of instruction and practice. Swimming instructors may work at indoor and outdoor public pools, private clubs, or at summer camps.

The future looks good for lifeguards, swimming instructors, and pool managers. There are more recreational and tourist facilities today than ever before. Qualified lifeguards and others are needed to teach and protect swimmers and to maintain pools.

The jobs at outdoor pools and beaches are seasonal in certain areas of the country. In warm weather areas, these jobs may be year round. Indoor pools usually are open to members and guests throughout the year.

For more information on lifeguards, swimming instructors, and pool managers, write to:

American Swimming Coaches Association
One Hall of Fame Drive
Fort Lauderdale, FL 33316

United States Lifesaving Association
c/o Chicago Park District
425 East 14th Street
Chicago, IL 60605
(312) 294–2332

People interested in becoming lifeguards, swimming instructors, or pool managers should also check with their local park districts or recreation departments. They hire summer workers for outdoor pools and year-round help for indoor pools.

Chapter 11
Hotel or Motel Manager

What keeps guests coming back again and again to a hotel or motel? The answer is clean rooms and good service. Hotel or motel managers oversee the daily operations of the place. They juggle many duties to keep their hotels or motels running smoothly.

Education, Training, and Salary

A high school education is required to be a hotel and motel manager. Often, a hotel or motel will also require some college courses in hotel-motel management. These may be taken evenings or on a part-time basis while working.

Those who want to become hotel managers may work part time in other hotel jobs to learn the business. This shows that they are willing to work. Some hotels and motels offer training programs that last up to three years.

Hotel and motel managers usually start at $18,000 to $25,000 a year, depending on the hotel or motel. With experience, they may earn $32,000 to $50,000.

Job Description

Managers' number-one concern is that guests are satisfied. A hotel's or motel's success depends on pleasing its guests.

Managers supervise the work of others, but in smaller hotels they may perform many of the jobs themselves. They check in guests, keep track of room vacancies, handle food orders, and keep all records. They hire housekeepers and custodians to do cleaning and maintenance.

In larger hotels, managers supervise the different departments: front desk, housekeeping, bellhops, maintenance, food and beverage manager, and others. These managers often have an assistant to help out. Managers or assistant managers work with the heads of each department, who pass information down to their workers.

Managers are often responsible for the finances of the hotel or motel. They must keep track of spending and balance the budget. They work closely with accountants to understand what money is available to the hotel or motel for advertising, fixing up the building, and other concerns.

Managers have a great deal of responsibility and often work long hours solving problems. They must always be available if needed to make a decision or handle a situation.

Some hotels hire sales managers who help advertise the hotel and its services to the public. The hotel may want to attract individuals, families, tourists, or conventions. Sales managers plan their ads or promotions to fit this target group. Suppose that a motel wants people to think of it as a family inn. It would advertise that it offers baby-sitting services, a family restaurant, pool, or game room.

If the hotel or motel includes a restaurant, the manager may be responsible for it, too. Or the restaurant may have a separate manager.

Did You Know?

The first hotel built for strictly hotel purposes was the City Hotel, of 70 rooms, opened in 1794 on Broadway, just below Wall Street, New York City. (Jefferson Williamson—The American Hotel).

The first hotel definitely recognized as a modern first-class hotel was the Tremont House in Boston, Massachusetts, which celebrated its opening with an elaborate dinner on October 16, 1829. It contained 170 rooms; the rate was $2 a day, including four meals. Travelers were permitted to rent a single room instead of having to double up with strangers. (Previously when guests retired for the night they did not know whom they might find beside them in the morning. Frequently three or four slept in one bed "spoon fash-ion." Women were sometimes "roomed" with men.) Other innovations at the Tremont House were a key for each room, a washbowl, a pitcher, and a free cake of soap for every guest, gaslights, and a fine supply of running water in the eight "bathing rooms" in the basement. (A description of the Tremont House. 1830)

The first motel was the Motel Inn built in 1924 on Neil Cook's property on the north side of San Luis Obispo and opened December 12, 1925. Arthur S. Heineman was the architect. Flashing lights altered the letters *H* and *M* preceding the letters *otel* to spell out motel and hotel. It had accommodations for 160 guests in individual chalets with garage, bathroom, and telephones. (Small cabins often were known as motels.)

Source: Joseph Nathan Kane, *Famous First Facts,* 4th ed. New York: H. W. Wilson, pp. 313, 400.

Managing a hotel or motel can be a seasonal job. This is true of ski facilities that might operate only in winter. These managers usually find other jobs for the rest of the year—possibly at summer resorts.

The hotel manager checks the uniform of this bellhop to ensure that customers get a good impression of the hotel.

Outlook for Jobs

Hotels and motels in a chain can differ in size. A manager in a small hotel often can advance by transferring to a larger one. Managers in large hotels usually have more responsibility and higher salaries. Managers who decide to go further in their careers may choose to aim for a job in the hotel headquarters.

As in other jobs, hard work and solid performance are the keys to moving up in the hotel and motel industry.

The outlook for jobs in hotel and motel management is excellent. Tourist and business travel are booming, and more hotels and motels are showing up across the country. Jobs also open up as managers transfer to other hotels and motels or retire.

Young people can apply to hotels or motels where they are interested in working. They can also check their school placement office and newspaper ads to see what openings are available.

For more information on hotel and motel managers, write to:

American Hotel and Motel Association
1201 New York Avenue, NW
Washington, DC 20005
(202) 289–3100

Council on Hotel, Restaurant and Institutional Education
311 First Street, NW
Washington, DC 20001
(202) 628–0038

Hotel Sales and Marketing Association International
1300 L Street, NW
Washington, DC 20005
(202) 789–0089

Interested people should also apply directly to hotels and motels to find out about job openings.

Chapter 12
Getting the Job:
Tips for the Reader

Starting Out

Whatever job you decide to go after, you want to do it to the best of your ability. And you can do this only if you have picked a job you enjoy and feel comfortable with. Be honest with yourself and begin your job search by knowing your talents and interests.

Rate Your Strengths

Write down on a piece of paper a few lines about yourself: what you like, what you dislike, what your favorite subject at school is, what your least favorite subject is, what bores you, what excites you.

Make a chart and list any jobs you have ever had. Include your supervisors' names, your work addresses, and the dates of employment. Now make a list of your hobbies or interests. Also list the schools you have attended and your extracurricular activities. This list would include clubs or teams you belong to. If you have done any volunteer work, be sure to list it. Finally, add to your list the names of any awards or prizes you have won. All this information helps you identify your strengths.

List Your Job Possibilities

List all the jobs in this book that sound interesting. Look at each job and see if you qualify. If a job you like requires extra training, write that down. Also check the publications in the back of this book and note the titles of any books or other materials that will tell you more about the jobs you like.

Look at your job list and your strengths list. See where they match up, and put a star by those jobs that would use your strengths.

Consult Counselors

Talk to a guidance counselor at your school about jobs that are open in your field of interest. Your state or local employment service can also help you.

Looking for Work

When you have settled on the jobs you would like, start looking for openings. Apply for as many jobs as you can—the more you apply for, the better your chance of finding one.

Research Find out everything you can about jobs you are applying for. The more information you have about jobs, employers, and employers' needs, the more impressive you will be in your interview.

Ads There are two types of newspaper classified ads: *help wanted* and *situation wanted.* A help wanted ad is placed by an employer looking for a worker to fill a specific job. It tells you the job, requirements, salary, company, and whom to contact. Or it is a blind ad, one that just has a post office box number. Answer the ad by letter or by phone, as directed in the ad. Follow up within two weeks with another phone call or letter if you have not heard from the employer.

A person looking for work can place a *situation wanted* ad. This ad tells the kind of work the person is looking for, why he or she qualifies, and when he or she could start working.

Networking Networking is letting everyone know what jobs you're looking for. Talk to people in your field of interest, friends, or relatives who might be able to help. Some good leads on jobs can be found this way. Follow up on what you learn with a phone call or letter.

Employment Services Check with the high school's or vocational school's placement service for job openings. State and local employment services often have job listings.

Classified Ads

Social Director Are you an outgoing person who likes to plan activities that are fun? We are a small senior citizens center that is looking for a social director to plan day trips, seasonal activities that will reach out to the community. Please send resume and salary requirements to C. Forney, 155 Grayson Place, Lilburn, GA.

Attention: waitresses: HIGH PAY! GREAT TIPS! SET YOUR OWN HOURS! Sound too good to be true? It's not! If you are a self-starter and are willing to work hard, call The Big Apple Deli at 555-2189 and ask for Steve.

OUTDOOR GUIDE NEEDED Large group is looking for exper. guide to lead two-week trip through Rocky Mountains. Call 555–1199 after 7:00 p.m.

Al's Diner wants you!!! Wanted p/t hostess, weekends. Will train. Call Al at 555–DINE.

Experienced groundskeeper seeks f/t position with landscaping firm. No work too hard. Own transportation. Ed, P.O. Box 500, Atlanta 30308.

Abbreviations

People who place classified ads often use abbreviated words to make an ad as short as possible. Read the classified ad section in your newspaper to become familiar with abbreviations. Here is a short list to help you now:

excel —— excellent		f.t.	
bnfts. —— benefits		or f/t — full time	
exp —— experience		emp. —— employment	
p.t.		gd. —— good	
or p/t — part time		refs. —— references	
h.s. —— high school		ext. —— extension	
grad —— graduate		req. —— required	
w. —— with		sal. —— salary	
avail. —— available			

Civil Service   Federal, state, and local governments offer some jobs in recreation. Find the civil service office near you and inquire. See the feature on the top of the next page. It explains more about civil service exams.

Unions   Find out about labor unions that may be involved with jobs in the field of community services. Check with union locals in your town; you can find phone numbers in the phone book.

Temporary Employment   Working on a temporary basis can lead to other jobs or to part-time or full-time work. Seasonal work is available for jobs such as lifeguard or recreation worker. Part-time work in a fast-food franchise or as a waiter or waitress is available.

Civil Service

Federal and state governments employ several million workers. In order to get a government job, you must first check with the Federal Job Information Center or a state Department of Personnel office for an announcement concerning the type of job that interests you. The announcement describes the job as well as the education and experience that all applicants will need to be qualified for the job.

Once you know about a government job opening, you must fill out an application to take a civil service test. If your application is approved, you must then take and pass the exam. Exams are usually written, but may also be oral. Some exams include essays or performance tests. All exams are tailored to fit a specific job. An exam may cover such items as English usage, reasoning, or clerical or mechanical skills.

Applying in Person

Applying to a company in person can be a good idea. Call for an appointment and tell the human resources officer that you would like to have an interview. Some employers may ask that you send a letter or résumé first.

Sending Letters

Writing letters to companies can be an effective way to ask about jobs. Typed letters are preferred, but neat, handwritten letters are acceptable. Check the yellow pages or industry magazines at the public library for companies' addresses. The reference librarian can help you. Address letters to the company's personnel or human resources department. Send your résumé with the letter. Keep copies of all letters and follow up in two weeks with another letter.

Résumé

A résumé is a useful one-page outline of information about you that introduces you to a possible future employer. Based on your strengths list, it summarizes your education, work history, and skills.

You will enclose your résumé in letters you write to future employers. You also will take it with you to give to your interviewer. Look at the sample résumé on page 87 to see how a typical résumé looks.

Always put your full name, address, and phone number at the top of the résumé. Type the résumé, if possible, or write it by hand neatly. Then state your objective, or the job you are applying for. Put down any experience that shows you are a good worker. Volunteer work and part-time jobs tell an employer that you are always looking to help out and work hard. Put down your most recent job first.

Finally, include information about your education. You can also list any special skills, awards, or honors you have received.

Writing Letters

When you send your résumé in the mail, always attach a cover letter. Your letter will be short, no more than two or three paragraphs. It should come right to the point and lead the employer to your résumé.

Explain what job you are interested in, and include a short listing of your qualifications. Your letter should catch the employer's interest so that the employer wants to turn to your résumé. See the sample on page 88.

Mario Santo
222 West 57th Street
El Segundo, CA 55555
(818) 555–4321

Objective: Job as restaurant cook.

Experience
Have been cooking since I was eight years old. I have helped out in my family's restaurant after school and on weekends.

1990	Worked as a kitchen helper at The Coffee Cup Restaurant preparing fruits and vegetables for the cooks and cleaning up.
1988–present	Volunteered to cook hot dogs and hamburgers at Kiwanis fundraising picnic. Also cooked and helped out at annual Pancake Day fundraising.

Education
1989   Graduated Westside Vocational School.

Training
Completed two-week cooking class given by Creative Cuisine.

Attended seminar in "Cooking for Groups" given by park district.

References available upon request.

May 5, 1990
Elizabeth Mayo
4421 Oakwood
Lester, SC 33333

Ms. Wendy Marshell
Manager, Island Beach Health Club
111 Ocean Boulevard
Island Beach, SC 33333

Dear Ms. Marshell:

I am interested in a job as a fitness instructor in the Island Beach Health Club. I am looking for a full-time or part-time position starting in June 1991, when I graduate from high school.

I have a great deal of experience in exercise and sports. I was on my high school soccer, cross country, and track teams. I have taught aerobics for two years at the YMCA. I have studied physical fitness and have taken several courses at Long Beach General Hospital.

I am enclosing my résumé so you can see my education and work experience. I would be happy to meet with you and discuss any job openings Island Beach Health Club might have in the near future.

Sincerely,

Elizabeth Mayo

enclosure

Completing the Application Form

You may have to fill out an application form when applying for a job. (See the sample on pages 90 and 91.) This form asks for your education, experience, work history, and possibly other information.

The employer may mail an application form to you ahead of time or you may be asked to fill it in when you come for the interview.

Follow the instructions carefully and print or type information neatly. Neatness tells the employer that you care about work, can organize information, and that you can think clearly.

Have all information with you when you arrive. You may have to fill in salaries for past jobs, your social security number, the dates you worked, and your past supervisors' names, addresses, and phone numbers.

List your most recent jobs first, as you do on your résumé.

However, do not answer any question that you feel invades your privacy. Laws prevent an employer from asking about race, religion, national origin, age, marital status, family situation, property, car, or arrest record. Unless the question applies directly to the job, you do not have to answer it. (See "Know Your Rights.")

The Interview

How you present yourself in a job interview will tell the employer a lot about you. It can be the biggest single factor that helps an employer decide whether to hire you.

Before you go to the interview, sit down and prepare what you will say. Think of why you

APPLICATION FOR EMPLOYMENT

(Please print or type your answers)

PERSONAL INFORMATION   Date _____

Name _____ Social Security Number _____/ _____/ _____

Address _____
           Street and Number   City   State   Zip Code

Telephone number (_____) _____ – _____ (_____) _____ – _____
                       day   evening

Job applied for _____ Salary expected $ _____ per _____

How did you learn of this position? _____

Do you want to work _____ Full time or _____ Part time?

Specify preferred days and hours if you answered part time _____

Have you worked for us before? _____ If yes, when? _____

On what date will you be able to start work? _____

Have you ever been convicted of a crime, excluding misdemeanors and summary offenses?

_____ No _____ Yes

If yes, describe in full _____

Whom should we notify in case of emergency?

Name _____ Relationship _____

Address _____
           Street and number   City   State   Zip Code

Telephone number (_____) _____ – _____ (_____) _____ – _____
                       day   evening

EDUCATION

Type of School	Name and Address	Years Attended	Graduated	Course or Major
High School			Yes No	
College			Yes No	
Post-graduate			Yes No	
Business or Trade			Yes No	
Military or other			Yes No	

WORK EXPERIENCE (List in order, beginning with most recent job)

Dates From	To	Employer's Name and Address	Rate of Pay Start/Finish	Position Held	Reason for Leaving

ACTIVITIES AND HONORS (List any academic, extracurricular, civic, or other achievements you consider significant.)

_____

_____

PERSONAL REFERENCES

Name and Occupation   Address   Phone Number

_____

_____

_____

PLEASE READ THE FOLLOWING STATEMENTS CAREFULLY AND SIGN BELOW:

The information that I have provided on this application is accurate to the best of my knowledge and is subject to validation. I authorize the schools, persons, current employer, and other organizations or employers named in this application to provide any relevant information that may be required to arrive at an employment decision.

_____   _____

Applicant's Signature   Date

want the job, your experience, and why you qualify. Learn as much about the job and the company as possible. You can get information by reading through ads or brochures or by talking to employees. This will show that you are interested in the company's needs.

Make a list of questions you have. And try to guess what the interviewer will ask. You may ask if you can work overtime or if you can take courses for more training or education. Bring in any certificates or licenses you may need to get the job you want.

Dress neatly and appropriately for the interview. Make sure you know exactly where the interview will take place so you will be on time. Allow extra time to get there in case you are delayed by traffic or for some other reason.

Following Up

After the interview, thank the interviewer for his or her time and shake hands. If the job appeals to you, tell the person that you are interested.

When you get back home, send a letter thanking the interviewer for his or her time. Repeat things that were discussed in the interview. Keep a copy of it for yourself and start a file for all future letters.

Think about how you acted in the interview. Did you ask the right questions? Were your answers right? If you feel you should have done something differently, make notes so you can do better the next time.

If you do not hear from the company in two weeks, write a letter to the interviewer repeating your interest. You can also phone to follow up.

Know Your Rights: What Is the Law?

Federal   Under federal law, employers cannot discriminate on the basis of race, religion, sex, national origin, ancestry, or age. People aged forty to seventy are specifically protected against age discrimination. Handicapped workers also are protected. Of course, these laws protect only workers who do their job. Employers are not stopped from hiring workers who are not qualified or firing workers who do not perform.

State   Many states have laws against discrimination based on age, handicap, or membership in armed services reserves. Laws differ from state to state. In some states, there can be no enforced retirement age. And some protect people suffering from AIDS.

Applications   When filling out applications, you do not have to answer questions that may discriminate. Questions about whether you are married, have children, own property or a car, or have an arrest record do not have to be answered. An employer may ask, however, if you have ever been convicted of a crime.

At Work   It is against the law for employers to discriminate against workers when setting hours, workplace conditions, salary, hirings, layoffs, firings, or promotions. And no employer can treat a worker unfairly if he or she has filed a discrimination suit or taken other legal action.

Read Your Contract   Read any work contract you are given. Do not sign it until you understand and agree to everything in it. Ask

93

questions if you have them. If you have used an employment agency, before you sign a contract, settle on whether you pay the fee for finding a job or the employer does.

When Discrimination Occurs: What You Can Do

Government Help   Call the Equal Employment Opportunities Commission or the state Civil Rights Commission if you feel you've been discriminated against. If they think you have been unfairly treated, they may take legal action. If you have been unfairly denied a job, you may get it. If you have been unfairly fired, you may get your job back and receive pay that is owed you. Any mention of the actions taken against you may be removed from your work records. To file a lawsuit, you will need a lawyer.

Private Help   Private organizations such as the American Civil Liberties Union (ACLU) and the National Association for the Advancement of Colored People (NAACP) fight against discrimination. They can give you advice.

Sources

General Career Information

Career Information Center, 4th ed., 13 vols. Mission Hills, Cal.: Glencoe/Macmillan, 1990.

Harrington, Thomas, and O'Shea, Arthur, (eds.). *Guide for Occupational Exploration.* Circle Pines, Minn.: American Guidance Service, 1984.

Hopke, William E., et al. (eds.). *The Encyclopedia of Careers and Vocational Guidance.* 7th ed., 3 vols. Chicago: Ferguson, 1987.

United States Department of Labor. *Occupational Outlook Handbook.* Washington, D.C.: United States Government Printing Office, revised biennially.

Hospitality And Recreation

Cylowski, G. J. *Developing a Career in Sports and Athletics.* Longmeadow, Mass.: Movement Publications, 1987.

Humphers, Sandra. *Exploring Careers in the Hotel and Motel Industry.* New York: Rosen Publishing Group, 1983.

Wasserman, Steven. *Recreation and Outdoor Life Directory.* Detroit, Mich.: Gale Research Co., updated annually.

Witzman, Joe, and Block, Jack. *Food Service Careers Guide Book.* San Diego: Educator's Publications, 1987.

Witzman, Joe, and Block, Jack. *Who's Hiring in Hospitality.* San Diego: Educator's Publications, 1987.

Index